Caveman Art Teacher

by Jeff Dombek

CORN TASSEL PRESS
Columbia, Maryland

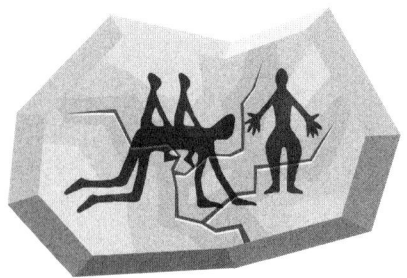

With love, to Diane, Kelly and Kristina

And to my students, who always teach me new ways to enjoy art

Special thanks to Keith H., Don S., Patrick C., Dave A., and Chip B., cavemen of the highest rank!

All rights reserved. No part of this book may be reproduced or transmitted in any form or by any means, electronic or mechanical, including photocopying, recording or by any information storage and retrieval system without written permission from the author, except for brief quotations in review. For information regarding permissions, write to: Corn Tassel Press, 9655 Corn Tassel Court, Columbia, MD 21046 U.S.A.

Caveman Art Teacher

Text and Illustrations copyright © 2004 by Jeff Dombek
All rights reserved
Printed in the United States of America

Book design and layout: Keith W. Heckert

ISBN 0-9752597-0-9

Contents

1. **Summer's End**
2. **I Hate Art**
3. **Dino-Disaster**
4. **Let's Try That Again...**
5. **Poster Contest**
6. **Time to Paint**
7. **Art Show**

1. Summer's End

Everything seemed so normal at first. Wearing our brand new school clothes in the hot August sun, we all waited nervously at the bus stop for the first day of school. Our parents couldn't help but smile and wave as the bus pulled away, the noisy engine drowning out the scratchy summer song of the nearby cicadas. When we finally arrived at school, the safeties were still putting up the American flag and yelling, "Walk!" at anyone who dared run in front of them. Upon entering my classroom, I stood in a very long line to order my chicken nugget lunch, and then we heard the principal's voice on the morning announcements welcoming everyone back from summer vacation. Like I said, it all seemed pretty normal. I was even a little nervous when we lined up to go to lunch and recess, just like I always am on the first day of school.

After recess was over, we sat quietly at our desks cooling ourselves while Miss Myers, our new second grade teacher, read to us from her rocking chair. When it was time for art, she said to the class, "Please line up behind your line leader with a hand at your hip, and a silent finger on your lip." I got in line and we headed down the hallway for Mrs. Lewis's art room. Upon arriving, everyone in the second grade at Fullerton Lane Elementary School knew we had a big problem. As we entered the art room, there was a *caveman* in the front of the room instead of Mrs. Lewis. Taller than any teacher I had ever seen, his hair looked like strands of black licorice. Animal skins hung like giant curtains from his shoulders and frayed dusty sandals were strapped to his feet. Behind him, the word "Caveman" was scrawled in big letters on the chalkboard. We sat down without saying a word. After a long uncomfortable silence, he muttered, "Mrs. Lewis at home...with baby... Caveman here to help."

What? What did he just say? Was this some kind of joke? I knew Mrs. Lewis was having a baby this summer, but *no one* told us kids that she wouldn't be back. Why didn't Miss Myers tell us about this *before* we came to art? Did she forget? Surely she must have known. As if losing our favorite art teacher wasn't bad enough, now we had a *caveman* for an art teacher. Was this really happening? Caveman reviewed the class rules, using hardly any words as he spoke. "Question...Raise hand." "Trash...Put here." "Wash hands...Go back table...Sit quiet." He adjusted his thick glasses and mumbled, "Mrs. Lewis...be back October 1st."

As he was "talking," I noticed that the arrangement of the art room looked mostly the same as it did last year, but there were a few puzzling changes. The supply counter, which previously held our collection of crayons, pencils, scissors, and glue, now had all sorts of rocks and fossils spread all over it. Additionally, the art tables were now labeled with different types of dinosaur names instead of having the names of artists, like last year and the year before. Even Mrs. Lewis's treasure box was different. No longer containing the usual stickers and toys, it was now stuffed with shark's teeth, bones, small fossils, gemstones, and what appeared to be dinosaur egg shells.

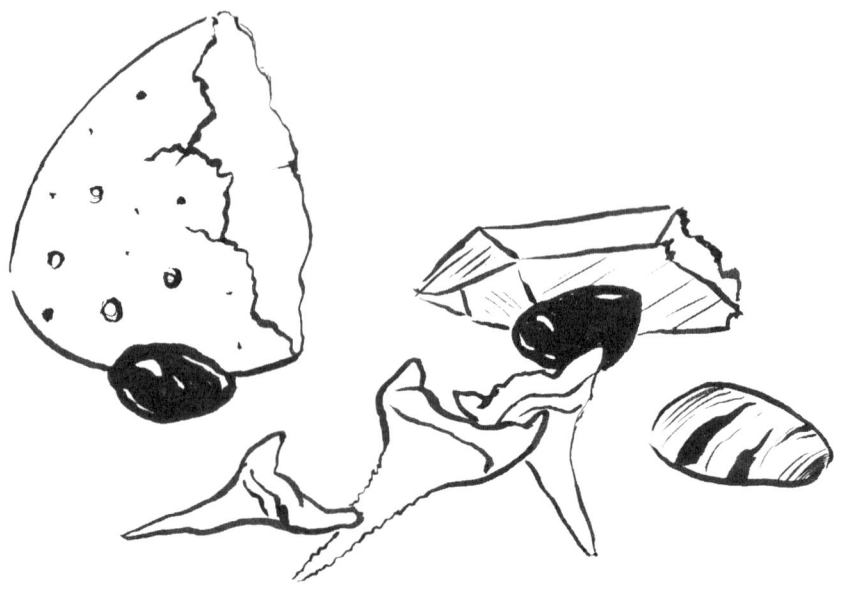

2. I Hate Art

Arriving home from school, I knew just how I would answer my Mom's annoying first question, the same one I'm asked every day the moment I step into the house. Sure enough, as soon as I walked through the door, she asked me for the thousandth time, "What did you do in school today, Amanda?"

"I had art class... with a *caveman*," I answered in a smug tone.

"Huh? What do you mean?" she said with a tilted head and puzzled face.

"I had art class with a caveman," I repeated louder.

"Oh, that's right. Mrs. Lewis must still be at home with her baby. Did you have a man art teacher for a substitute today?" she asked.

"I had art class with a caveman," I repeated slowly for the third time.

"Oh sweetheart, isn't Mrs. Lewis coming back?" she prodded.

"Not 'till October 1st," I stomped. "My art teacher is a caveman. I *hate* art."

The next evening was a PTA meeting and Back-To-School Night. The parents were asking all kinds of questions about the new art teacher.

"What university did he attend?"

"Is he certified?"

"Is he the best candidate for the job?"

"Well," answered Mr. Kim, our principal, "Personnel is verifying his college transcripts. They also tell me he's our strongest art substitute; he broke five pencils during his written examination at the Board of Education. He'll be our art teacher for the next month or so." Afterwards, the parents met all the teachers, including our strange new art teacher. "Nice to meet you and welcome to our school, Mr.

Caveman, is it?" someone said. "Call me Caveman, please," he answered, shaking hands with all the parents. "Where did you attend college?" my mother politely inquired. He simply pointed to a tattered blue and yellow baseball cap on his desk with the words "Fightin' Blue Pterodacs" on the front and then to the framed degree hanging on the wall which said "Bachelor of Fine Arts" in fancy letters with the name "Caveman" underneath.

3. Dino-Disaster

Entering the art room the following week, our class was excited to see a giant pile of reddish brown clay sitting on the supply counter. Caveman had put pictures of dinosaurs all over the chalkboard. Standing beside his desk, he cupped his hands together and simply said, "Okay, today, we make dinosaur from clay. Get clay... Have fun!" Puzzled, we looked at one another as if we had just been handed the keys to a fully-stocked candy store at dinnertime, and then the whole class rushed to the big pile of clay on the counter.

"Look at all that clay!" shouted Jimmy.

"Don't take it all," warned Toby, "Gimme some!"

Everyone was pushing and yelling, and taking *way*

too much clay for themselves. By the time I got to the pile, there wasn't any clay left at all, just a muddy counter top. Caveman told Jimmy, who had a lump of clay the size of a soccer ball, to share some of his clay with me. If Mrs. Lewis had been there, the whole

class would have gone to time-out. Everyone except me, of course.

Even after everyone had settled down to work with their own clay, art class never did improve. Legs and arms and heads were falling off of clay dinosaur bodies all around the room. I saw Alice crying because the wings on her pterodactyl kept breaking. My tyrannosaurus kept tipping over and breaking at the tail. An occasional stegosaurus snout flew through the air in frustration. There was clay on the floor, mud all over the tables, and even some clay stuck in Bobby's curly hair. The class was so noisy that the other teachers kept peering into the art room as they walked by. I read Mrs. McGinn's lips as she mouthed, "Oh my heavens!" while peeking through the glass door. Mrs. Brown just laughed and then covered her face with her hands while shaking her head. Things were *way* out of control, and the whole class knew it.

A few moments later, Caveman's face turned red.

He was frozen in place, slowly staring at everyone, and at no one at all.

Suddenly his thick eyebrows formed an angry expression over his eyes as he snarled loudly,

"Stop!"

The room went completely silent. You could even hear the clock ticking on the wall. We were toast.

"Put back clay, *now*," he growled slowly.

"Can I wash my-"

"No! Sit Jimmy!"

No one dared to move an inch until Caveman dismissed their table to wash at the sink. What a mess. Our dinosaurs looked ridiculous, and so did our mud-caked art room. Art was a disaster. It was once my favorite class, but now I hated art.

4. Let's Try That Again...

By the following week, I wasn't even looking forward to Tuesday, which is my art day. Surprisingly, the next art class went much more smoothly than the "Dino-Disaster" we had a week earlier. Caveman showed us in the beginning of class how to join pieces of clay so they would stay together. He began by scratching the clay first, adding water, and *then* pushing the pieces together. It really worked! He also chose table captains to help pass out the clay this time, just like Mrs. Lewis always had done. Even Jimmy had a dinosaur with legs that didn't break off, although I couldn't tell if his sculpture was a dinosaur or a giant hamster. The wings on Alice's pterodactyl were huge, and her sculpture was the biggest in the class. My T-rex was the best I'd ever made, and the tail looked as sturdy as ever. At clean-up, no one had to remove clay from their hair, either. Caveman seemed noticeably happier.

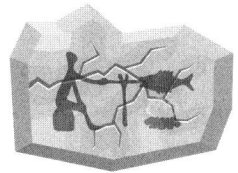

5. Poster Contest

At the next PTA meeting, Mrs. Little asked about the second grade poster contest held each year at the volunteer firehouse. She looked worried. "I'm on the refreshments committee, but I don't even know if the kids have started the artwork for the show yet. Jonathan tells me the only projects they've done so far this year have been made in clay." Mrs. Little continued, "Has anyone informed Mr. Caveman about this upcoming special event? He only has one week to get the children ready. Oh, and by the way, the sign up sheet for baking cookies is on the front table. Be sure to indicate the kind of cookies you'll be bringing." "Thank you, Mrs. Little," reassured Mr. Kim. "I'll make sure Mr. Caveman knows about the

Fire Safety Poster Contest."

The next day, Mr. Kim called Caveman into his office. "Caveman," he said, "I'm sorry for the late notice, but we'll need Fire Safety posters in one week for the reception at the firehouse." Caveman looked puzzled. "Caveman teach clay in art...not know how to paint," he stammered. "Well," the principal demanded, "you'll have to learn how. I'll need those posters by October 1st."

Caveman went to the library to check out some books on painting. He read for hours. After some practice back in the art room, he finally decided on how the posters would be made. The children would learn how to paint "fire" by mixing red and yellow paints.

6. Time to Paint

The next day at school, we put on our smocks before we lined up to go to art class. For the first time all year, the art room smelled like paints. I was very excited. "Today," announced Caveman, "make picture for poster contest. Fire Safety contest in one week. Do your best!" Caveman then demonstrated how to mix the colors to make a fiery orange. Once the paints and paper were passed out to the tables, we got right to work. Everyone did their best because it was a contest and our parents would be at the firehouse to see all of our paintings.

After finishing our paintings, we put them on the drying rack. Everyone except Jimmy, that is. Jimmy painted his arm and hand orange to look like fire, but he never painted *anything* on his paper. Jimmy is *always* getting into trouble. He went to time-out after spending forever at the sink washing himself. You could still see some orange on his arm even after he tried to wash it off. For my poster, I painted a picture of my family waiting on our driveway with the words GeT oUT anD StAY OuT! at the top of my paper. It looked pretty good to me. Caveman smiled at me as I sat quietly at my table waiting for everyone else to wash their hands. "Go pick prize...you nice girl...you do nice picture..." he said. I looked in the treasure box and picked out a giant shark's tooth and put it in my pocket. As the class lined up to return to Miss Myers' room, Caveman smiled and said, "Caveman very happy... you paint lovely posters... very proud of you today." Miss Myers beamed at hearing such a good report about her class. She was so happy, in fact, that no one wanted to spoil her good mood by tattling about Jimmy's orange arm.

7. Art Show

The next time I saw Caveman was on the first day of October. There was frost on the grass that morning, but it was sunny and warm after school when I saw him putting all of our paintings in his pickup truck. He placed two big rocks on top of them so they wouldn't blow away as he drove to the firehouse.

Well, tonight was the big night – the art show at the firehouse. I could hardly wait. The fire chief would select posters for first, second, and third prize and then hang a puffy ribbon on each. Parents, teachers and kids would all be there, with lots of cookies to choose from afterwards.

My family and I arrived at the firehouse just in

time. The fire chief had the three ribbons in his hand and was making a final inspection before hanging them on the winning posters. Stepping up to the microphone, he announced, "All of these paintings are so wonderful, and each one shows the importance of fire safety, but three posters have especially caught my eye." He paused, and then continued, "In first place, Tammy Truman." Everyone cheered, but we all knew she would win first prize. Her pictures are always *so* perfect. "In second place," he continued as my stomach fluttered, "Jonathan Little." Cheers went up again. Then he walked over to Caveman, who whispered something to the fire chief while looking right at me. My heart was pounding! "And in third place," he bellowed, "Amanda Denison." I was stunned. My face and ears felt hot and tingly. I had never won a ribbon in any contest before - *ever!* Caveman was smiling at me from across the room. It was then that I finally realized that you really *could* learn a lot from a caveman, and I didn't hate art anymore. Then I felt sad because I realized today was Caveman's last day as substitute art teacher at our school. But not too sad that I couldn't enjoy a few cookies with my friends.

Right before it was time to leave, I heard some parents yell, "Surprise!" They had made a giant cake for Caveman. In letters made with blue and yellow frosting, it said "Thank You Mr. Caveman!" Our P.E. teacher was rushing to hang a giant banner that said "We'll Miss You Mr. C!" But just as she got to the top of the stepladder, she slipped and fell. The firefighters rushed to check her ankle, which hurt so badly she couldn't walk. They wrapped her ankle in ice, and that's when I heard Mr. Kim say, "Mr. Caveman, would you happen to be available to teach P.E. for a few days...?"